Man Laws:

Don't Break 'em

Chris James and Manswell T. Peterson

www.ManswellPeterson.com

Man Laws: Don't Break 'em

Copyright © 2013 by OmegaMan Publishing

ISBN: 978-0988435179

Cover art designed by Gregory Graphics.

All rights reserved. No part of this book may be reproduced or transmitted in any form or by any means, electronic or mechanical, including photocopying, recording, or by any information storage and retrieval system, without permission in writing from the copyright owner.

This is a work of fiction. Names, characters, places and incidents either are the product of the author's imagination or are used fictitiously, and any resemblance to any actual persons, living or dead, events, or locales is entirely coincidental.

This book was printed in the United States of America.

To order additional copies of this book, contact:

www.Amazon.com

ACKNOWLEDGMENTS

CHRIS JAMES

To my Parents Dan and Elaine James: Thanks for always supporting me in everything that I do. I love you both so much.
Melanie, Monica, Dan IV, and Bruce thanks for always being there for me. We have seen some Great things in our lifetimes, and much more is to come.

Rhonda Amerson: Thanks for helping me put this together. Words will never say enough.

Thanks to my Dream Team for always holding me down, and a bond that will never be broken!!!

My church family Mt. Pilgram...Thanks for always blessing me and being there.

Victor Sibley Thanks for laughing and helping me with some of the Craziest Man Laws.

my Albany, Georgia family...much love to you all

To my Crimson Tide family, thanks for always being there. The memories will always be dear to me "Roll Tide Roll"

To all of my Dougherty High Trojans...Keep representing the BEST!!!

To all of my aunts, uncles, cousins thanks for always loving me and supporting me.

To my daughter Caden, daddy loves you!!!

To my brothers in law Jerome and Tim thanks for the support!!!

To my S.E.C family thanks for Fall football!!!

To anyone that I might have left out, blame it on my head and not my heart, I love you all!!!

To Manswell T. Peterson thanks for giving me a chance to show the world my talent.

To my Facebook family...I love you all...Stay on top as always.

To all of my personal friends, forgive me...there are just too many to name. Thanks for all that you have done!!!

Chris James

ACKNOWLEDGEMENTS

MANSWELL T PETERSON

I want to thank the following people for all their support and help.

Greg—Best cover designer in the World. As always Great Job!!!

In gratitude and love to my silent seven who were there with me from the beginning. You all kept asking for the return, and now I can say it is here…I hope I make you all Proud!!!

To all my fans from MySpace to Facebook, thank you for your emails, even the crazy ones. LOL.

To anyone I might have forgotten, I thank you also. Let's shock the world.

I love you all. Drop me a line some time.

Manswell T. Peterson

www.ManswellPeterson.com

As you begin this joyful journey into what and how men think, please remember that this is for your enjoyment and pleasure. It is so often that we as men see what some other men are doing and it drives most of us crazy. Ladies, please understand that most men will never ever say some of these things out loud because it should be a norm for most of us. Unfortunately, the time has come for us to break our silence and tell these guys what they are doing wrong and how. Welcome to the "Official Man Law Book!"

***The purpose of our Man Laws, are not designed to attack any person or any group of people, but to educate them on the things that we as a universe, have gotten away from. Things that our fathers and grandfathers as men, would not have accepted back in the days, have become acceptable....skinny jeans, riding on motorcycles with other dudes, etc....the men today are getting soft! Time to get it right, fellas! ***

We felt there was no need to waste any time and we will jump right into the man law violations and help you understand and picture some things we have seen.

*****

If you own a yard, and you have a lawn service to do your yard work for you, you can never bring the guy that's cutting your grass lemonade or sweet tea. Only Gatorade, energy drinks, or bottled water is accepted. Bringing another man lemonade or sweet tea with ice in it?!?! Come on bruh!

This violation has been going on for too long in the summer months and since we are releasing in the summer, we felt it was necessary to have this one lead off. Way too many guys are bringing lawn men stuff they shouldn't be. As a matter of fact, let him burn up in the heat, sit in the shade or something, but never bring him anything other than what we have listed above, anything else is a clear violation and you will lose your "Man Card" for six months.

*****

Certain nicknames men should NEVER answer to ...PEACHES, STRAWBERRY, JUICY, REFEREE, DELICIOUS, LIL BIT, COCO… If you know any man that answers to, or goes by the aforementioned nicknames, you must immediately inform him that he has about 10 minutes to come up with a new nickname or just simply go by his government name. If he has a screwed up name, tell him to blame his mother. He can go by the first syllable... for example, if his government name is "Jorenovice", he can just go by "Jo" or "JoJo". Don't leave yourself as an open target for jokes fellas!

Can you imagine you and the fellas sitting in the park after playing some basketball and some ladies walk up to you and your boys, they introduce themselves and you have to call out a name like Sweetness or Juiicy??!?!!? No, neither can we...smh. Picture how that looks, yeah we know!!!!!

*****

No man is to ever put Neosporin on another man's cut for him. That's too intimate. Now pouring alcohol or peroxide on it is acceptable, because that's forcing the injured guy to man up. So the manly values are upheld in that situation to an extent. But, if you are the man with Neosporin in your gym bag...slap yourself for having it in there in the first place. Let him rub some dirt on it and let his lady take care of it when he gets to his house.

*****

Anytime a man has the fireplace going in his house while another man is present, there must be a woman or kid(s) present, or the power has to be out. It can't just be those men there… otherwise the guest male must leave immediately.

Please whatever you do make sure that the women equal the amount of men, if there are two women…then it should be two men. If you go to your homeboy's house and he has a fireplace going and his lady is there, back out of the door as fast as you can, staying would be a major violation of the man laws. Don't be hanging around to see if she got a girlfriend coming over. The answer is NO!!!!

*****

No man is to ever get jealous and ask his homeboy "when will you make time for me? You're always finding time to do other things."...Something about that homeboyship ain't right. We need to have a meeting bruh," Coach wants to see you in his office...oh and bring your playbook.

If after your homeboy sees you have company and says the above...delete his number, treat him like the child support people or the people from one of those Rent-a- center places. You are to disavow him right there on the spot and Never take his calls or texts again.

*****

No man is to EVER have another man's picture programmed in his phone to pop up when he texts or calls. NO! I know what you look like bruh! No need for all of that!

If one of your boys has this done to his phone, pick up the nearest brick. Hit him in the forehead and break his phone and let him know to stop putting dudes pictures in his phone. Before you ask, NO, you can't have your brothers, nephews, or cousins' pictures either.

*****

You can tell if a man is a true athlete by how he holds the football when he runs. If you hold the football like a loaf of bread, chances are you don't know how to throw a spiral. #Sad...

There are no words for this except sad, sad, sad!!! Most young boys are taught this early in their lives. Ladies, if he tells you that he was this and that in high school or college, and you see him barely holding the football. Ask for some pictures...every sports person has some, one or two pictures of themselves in uniform.

*****

When going bowling, no man is to ever roll the ball with both hands, legs opened wide (picture that) #getyourweightup.

Do we have to even explain this one…no…ok, moving on!!!!

*****

When you are at a restaurant celebrating with the guys…you NEVER….Ever do this. Look at the menu and after a few minutes look at your homeboy and say "I can't make up my mind, what are you having?"

*****

"Hey friend" is not a proper way to address another man.

If you got a friend that does this, and you warn him about this and he does it again. You must punch him in the jaw…right or left side, then go home and take a 20 minute shower to wash any germs off that might have contaminated you.

No man is to ever place his hand on his chest and cough (picture that!). Even if you are alone at home, you should pound your chest until a lung comes up or something. Do this in a public place and watch how your boys look at you.

*****

If you're out at a club/lounge with a woman and she asks you to hold her drink for a second and the drink is fruity and has all kinds of decorations… you must look as tough as possible while holding the aforementioned fruity drink. If she left that drink with you and she is dancing with another man, you are to put the drink down. Because, if this is your girl, she won't be for long…sorry, just telling you the truth.

*****

OMG !!! OMG!!! OMG!!! Is not something a man should type, unless he's referring to the song. Go look in the mirror in your house and say that out loud…yeah, we thought so. If you look crazy saying it, how do you think you look typing it on Facebook. No exceptions

*****

If you close your eyes while hugging another man, that means you secretly adore/lust after him. Don't secretly adore another man <in my Direct TV commercial voice>

Yeah, you know that one that always wants to hug you after church…smh

*****

If you squeezed out too much lotion into your hand, you cannot tell another hand another man to get some of the lotion because you got too much. That lotion has to go back into the bottle or go to waste. No exceptions!…

If one of your boys tries this, throw him a towel, but never reach your hand out and take the lotion. You have just crossed a line that can never be undone.

As you can see, some of these should be common sense. How many of you right now are shaking your head because you have done one or more of these. Don't worry, we are shaking our heads laughing at you because you didn't know any better.

Ladies have you seen your man do some of these things? Now you are wondering, aren't you? Don't be too hard on him; maybe he just didn't have anyone to help guide him along the way.

*****

No man is to call another man to say, "I'm calling you just to give you a wake-up call"....hell naw!..instead, it's supposed to be..."Wake your a$$ up bruh!"...say it with authority.

After you have made the call "Once", you hang up, not even giving him a chance to say nothing!!! If you hold on to the phone, you have just committed a major violation and should be publicly whipped thirty times.

*****

No man should ever have to have a "night light" just to be able to sleep.

If this is you…go skydiving without the parachute. How are you going to protect the house when you are afraid of the dark!!??!!??!! You are the type of man to tell your lady to go check on the noises that you hear downstairs.

*****

No man is to throw an all-male pool party, because it's supposed to be a "bonding" activity…leave town right now. Don't pack your clothes or nothing…just get in your car and start driving until we tell you that we are tired.
*****

When you're on an interview, and the employer asks you "Why should we hire you", no man is to ever bust out in a cheer, to explain why…nor should he smack his lips together before answering. (Picture that)

*****

No man is to ever use lotion with any type of fruit on the bottle.

Do we really have to explain why no guy should be walking around smelling like apples, pears, or berries!?!?!?! Ok, think about that next time, and just be an ashy dude.

*****

No man is to ever blind-fold another man, unless he's in the mafia and holding him for ransom. Yes, you really need to be in the mafia to do this.

There is something very strange and wrong about a guy blind folded by another guy. If the person you thought was in the mafia starts to giggle, you are required to break out of whatever bondage that has been used and whip that guy's tail. No dude should be giggling at all in this situation.

*****

If you're in a house full of dudes, and you hear some Luther Vandross or some Maxwell come on, you must immediately get up, and go to your car....no stops to use the bathroom or nothing.

*****

Stop at a local gas station or restaurant but never be the one that goes to the bathroom. You might come out and find someone smiling at you and asking you to dance. Now you must punch this person in the face twice and kick them three times. Just leave the house to be safe, because every guy that left will know that you went to bathroom and assume you wanted to stay. Not a good look dude.

*****

No Man is to use tissue to wipe his eyes when crying...if a man has to cry, he must make the ugliest face possible.

Our advice on this is to cry alone and that way no one sees you, but if you got to do it and your nose starts to run...wipe it with your shirt but keep the ugly face.

*****

If you catch your young son looking at a Playboy magazine or Hustler, or any of those magazines, you must get on him, but deep down on the inside wanting to give him a high-five. If you catch him playing with a Barbie doll, then you

replace it with the Playboy and Hustler magazines

While the argument you will have with your wife/girlfriend about you replacing the dolls for the magazine might be crazy and loud…it will be worth for you and your son later.

*****

No Man is to use his index finger to tell another man to "come here". The only time a finger wave or wag is to be used, is if you just blocked somebody's shot in basketball and you're imitating Mutumbo.

If a guy does this to you, you are required to slap him so hard that he loses two days from his memory. You do this so he will never think about you this way never ever again.

*****

Men drinking margaritas and watching football do not mix, at all. (Saw it at Chili's and I was disappointed). They really thought they looked cool, but honestly most of the women were talking …grab a beer and never be doubted again. You can never look hard drinking a margarita and watching football.

*****

If another man asks you to tie his shoes for him, you must then proceed to uppercut him at a 180 degree angle. If you don't knock out at least two teeth, he must get hit again until the count goes up to two. No man should ever ask you to do that unless he is your granddad…

*****

When you are at a party and it's time to open gifts, when someone opens a gift, no man can say, "Awwww"...slap yourself. If you don't, I am sure there will be people there willing to do it for you.

*****

Dudes kill us being groupies...With that being said, we gotta bring out a couple Man Laws

about this.....{a} No Man is to ever get excited about an Usher concert or an Usher party....The only "Usher" a man should get excited about, is the "Usher" who brings him a fan in them hot country churches. {b} The only Tyrese that a man should get excited about, is Tyrese Jackson, who actually is the daddy of that baby, and not him .If you are running around jumping cause you got tickets, we hope you break your big toe and can't go.

*****

If a man comes up to you and puts his hand on your shoulder and talks softly, either one of two things about to happen....1. He's about to shank you or 2. He's about to try you.....With that being said, you are permitted to break his wrist and not feel guilty about it. Run after you do this because you don't know how many friends he has there.

*****

If you've just finished working out, and your workout partner says, "Let's hit the showers"....and this workout partner is not a woman, you may wanna wait 'til you get home. Leave the gym as fast as you can ok, don't look back...just go straight to your car and leave.

*****

If another man attempts to tickle you, you must bloody his nose, quick!

Any questions?!?!? We hope not...

*****

No man is to ever call another man during booty calls hours just to have convo....you're tying up my line! Wait, why in the heck are you calling me late at night anyway, hang up in his face and go back to watching tv.

*****

No man is to ever write XOXOXOXO.....unless you're drawing up football or basketball plays. If you do this on Facebook and we catch you, we will bust you in the nose.

*****

No two men should ever be sitting up at Cold Stone Creamery eating ice cream together....wrong kinda friendship...someone needs to go out in the mall and look at ladies fast.

*****

No man is to make his woman pump gas while he sits in the car and waits. Get yo lazy butt out of the car and pump that gas before you are riding the bus again. SMH...

*****

No man is to sit there and watch his woman get disrespected by another person, no matter if the guy or woman is twice his size. You better kick 'em in the knee or something, or you'll never hear the end of it.....that is all. If you kick them and they laugh at you, punch em in the throat and run to the car, dragging your lady behind you.

*****

If another man calls you to come over and help him decorate his new place, then you must immediately terminate the friendship. No more emails, texts, or phone calls are allowed, as a matter of fact, changing your number is not a bad idea.

*****

If another man calls you and tells you to meet him in the following places, then you might wanna run......Bed Bath & Beyond, any Italian restaurant, a hotel room that's in the same city he lives in, the movies, etc...Don't ignore the signs bruh!, please don't Ignore the signs!!!!

*****

No man is to ever call his homeboy over to come and watch a movie with him....that's grounds for a broken friendship. Watch it by yourself, you are never ever to do this...

*****

No man is to call his boy and apologize for an earlier argument. Just grab a case of beer, and no need for an apology.

*****

The rest shall be worked away as the beers disappear, never ever call and say "Man, I am sorry for our argument." It should be the last time you talk to your homeboy, he might not take your call again.

*****

No man is to ever buy another man a card, balloons, nor candy for his birthday...all that is required is a case of beer, a bottle of anything but wine, or some strippers...lol.

If you buy any of those things for your homeboy and he knocks you OUT!!! You deserved it...

*****

If a man calls you and sings happy birthday to you, you must immediately hang up the phone, drive or fly to his place, then punch him in the face, five times.

Yeah, you got some guys out there calling their male friends and Singing...yes, singing Happy Birthday...WOW!!!!!

*****

If you're in the shower and your homeboy rings your doorbell, either 1 of 2 things must happen. 1) They must wait outside until you finish and put something on, or 2) You unlock the door, and he must wait 30 seconds until he comes in, therefore giving you time to get back in the bathroom. I am not about to bust my butt running on a wet floor…better yet, sit in your car until I come out…yeah, that's better.

*****

No man is to tell another man, "Let's do lunch", unless money is involved, and he must change up how he words it.

Are we the only ones to see something wrong with this?!?!? Oh, ok…

*****

No man is to ever tell another man that he missed a loop with his belt....Why the hell you lookin' there in the first place??

Don't try and sell us on that BULL**** that is about to come out of your mouth, you should never be looking at a man's midsection.

*****

No man is to refer to his roommate as his roomie....matter fact, that word shouldn't be in your vocabulary....bestie shouldn't be either.

Think about what you are saying and how it sounds coming out of a guy's mouth!!! Yeah, we bet you won't ever say that again.

*****

If you're at a Trey Songz or any R&B artist concert, (in which you must attend with a woman), whenever the artist is singing a part of the song and he holds the mic out to the audience for them to finish the part, no man is to ever sing it. Matter fact, he must be mute at the time.

Get caught singing, even worse than that, you are up singing the part at the top of your lungs. Not a good look at all.

*****

No man is to ever ask his homeboy for some socks, because his feet are cold.

If your raggedy feet are cold let them stay cold and deal with it, but the moment you ask for socks…the game has changed forever.

*****

No man is to ever cry at a concert; unless it's a gospel concert and he done caught the Holy Ghost, even when you catch the Holy Ghost make sure you are not sitting there like a well known comedian and just crying a river. Suck it up and get yourself together.

*****

No man is to move to a different spot to take a picture so the lighting can bring out his eye color. You better just deal with the picture you got and keep it moving. I wish you would ask one of us to take another picture of you because your eyes will look better. You better hope we don't pop you in your jaw!!!

*****

No man is to plan a trip to the cabins with his boys, unless women will be available...

What were you expecting us to do?!?!?!?! Play spades with each other during the trip? Are you for real?!?!?!?! There is only so much time you should want to spend around all dudes anyway....smh

*****

In a pickup football, no man is to voluntarily wanna hike the ball. Everyone else wants to be a quarterback or catch a touchdown and you are running to the ball already bending over. Picture that...remember everyone is looking at you.

*****

No man is to post statuses about how the women on Housewives of Atlanta are trippin', nor how he hate he missed True Blood that night.

Really...Did you really just post that for all 2,439 of your friends to see it?!?!?!? No, it doesn't

make you look cool to your lady friends posting it.

*****

No man is to write a note on Facebook, talking about how good of friends his homeboys are.....kinda suspect, bruh....smh!!!

We don't care how long you have known your boys, never and we mean NEVER post such an emotional things anywhere, Especially on any Social Media site.

*****

No man is to EVER take a picture of himself with his lips puckered out, with him looking back at it nor with his shirt off, just to use it as a profile pic...PUNCH YOSELF twenty times real hard!!

Go to your mirror and do it….do you see how crazy you look doing that?!?!? Now punch yoself five more times for doing it again….

*****

If any man's car breaks down, even if he doesn't know what the hell he's doing, he must at least lift up the hood and act like he knows what the problem is.

Get yourself out of the car…let the steam hit you in the face; you just hang out under the hood until the tow truck comes to get you.

*****

No man is to have a profile pic of another man with his shirt off….athlete or not. Having a pic of T.O. with his shirt off as your default is disturbing.

Really?!?!?! With all the pictures of cheerleaders or dance members from the N.B.A or NFL…you put a half naked dude up…walk off the nearest curb into traffic and keep going until a Mack Truck hits you…

*****

No man is to run and leave his lady behind, when he hears gunshots....they better hit the floor. Now if you must run, drag her behind you…as long as she is still there, you are good. Even if she breaks the high heel shoes she has on, you saved her life and now she owes you BIGTIME!!!!

*****

No man is to call a friend over to remove a rodent from his house.

Yeah, it has happened before. If this is you, you need to go enlist in the armed forces or something...because you need to be broken down and made all over again.

*****

If you happen to be in the stands with your chest painted with your boys, no two men are to hug to celebrate a touchdown...dude you don't have a shirt on and now you are hugging another man..."WITHOUT a shirt on"...picture it...now punch yoself in the face...twice.

*****

No man is to ever chew gum and clean his nails at the same time.
Any questions?!?!?! Ok, we can move along now...

*****

If you and a nice young lady decide to do the do, and afterwards, she says, "Oh. Man, what did I just do?" "I am so mad at myself!".....you are to immediately lay her back down and give her

Round 2, and remind her why she did it the first time....lol....Take charge men!!

Repeat as necessary...she will get it.....LOL

*****

No man is to ever tell another man, that he has a shoulder for him to lean on. Bruh, you better go

and hug a tree. You are allowed to drive your homeboy to a tree...but not allowed to get out of your car while he is hugging said tree.

*****

No man is to ever cuff his hands and whisper into another man's ear...that's grounds for serious stab wounds...

Especially if you do this in a public place or at a party. How far is your nearest hospital? You will be going there for a visit.

*****

Two men should never have their shirts off simultaneously in a room, unless they're getting dressed to go somewhere...and they must be on opposite sides of the room. One of you should put your shirt on fast so that no mistakes are assumed if a lady comes by.

*****

No two men are to ever wrestle shirtless, unless they're in the WWE!!! If you are doing this just for fun and you are above the age of 12...go grab a stick and hit yoself...

*****

No man is to ever tell another man "Nice Abs" or "Nice shoulders", No compliments.

Any questions on this one could cause you to lose your Man card for a year or more.

*****

No man is to ever give another man the phone fingers and say, "Call Me" silently. This could cause a chair to come crashing against your head…doesn't matter where, and it must be done right away.

*****

No man is to ever complain about the type of alcohol another man is buying; when he didn't put in on it...You have no say so.

Just drink and be merry…and hopefully they will let you have a refill.

*****

Talking during the 4th quarter of a tight game will get you cut. If YOU EVER talk during this time an emergency room visit is in your future…you might get carried by six. Talking is only allowed during bathroom breaks and No, you can't come to the bathroom with me.

*****

No man is to ever touch another man's belt, belt loop, or pants period, while he is wearing them. The only pass is if he's drunk and you're taking his car keys out of his pocket...that's it. Please read this again, you will not get a pass on this one at all. If you are not drunk and you do this...please have your insurance card ready!!!

*****

No man is to ever get mad with his homeboy because he didn't call him back last night. Only acceptable if he owes him money, but you still need to just catch up with him later. How does that look when you see him and you say "You didn't call me back last night?!?!?!" Yeah, you know we are telling the truth.

*****

No man is to ever sip on wine while watching the game....major violation!!! If you girl offers you a glass of wine, you need to turn it down and ask for a beer or something stronger. If nothing else is available, you need to just grab a coke and have a smile.

*****

No man is to ever drop 5 stacks on a makeup bag if his butt is 5 stacks in debt. Sorry ladies, it has to wait. Dude if you know you are behind on your bills and child support, you have no right to be dropping money on a lady that might not be around in 4 or 5 months. Go walk in front of a city bus with no brakes…

*****

Homeboys or not, no two men are to ever share a love seat. Naw bruh, u gotta sit on the floor. This is non-negotiable so don't even start trying to talk your way on to the love seat.

*****

only acceptable during sporting events, specifically track....and you gotta be fast.

SO if you don't have blazing speed...No tights!!!
No one should ever be able to see a do-rag on your head...NEVER!!!!

*****

No man is to ever have a slow song as their ringtone. Cause what would it look like if your homeboy is calling you and "There Goes My Baby" comes on?? That ain't right.
Can you imagine how that lady will look at you when you try to explain that wasn't a lady calling you but one of your boys!!!! Yeah...we know....lol

*****

No man is to ever cry, when his homeboy walks down the aisle at his wedding.....even if it's his brother.....Man Up! What kind of relationship did y'all have??!!

Next thing you know, you will be asking can you go on the Honeymoon with them. C'mon Son!!!!!

*****

If you want your son to get into music, lay out a bunch of instruments in front of him......If he goes to the drums, he has a strong personality...he'll be a ladies' man. If he goes towards the saxophone, he's laid back, like a smooth operator. If he goes and picks up the tambourine, you better go and tackle him immediately, and introduce him to football.

Bust that tambourine against his head and never let him see it again...pop him in the head again, just to be sure.

*****

No man should ever apply for the following jobs....{a} Hooters Girl {b} Cheerleading Coach {c} Go-Go Dancer {d} Showgirl in Vegas {e} Body-building contest judge {f} Bartender in an All Male's Club {g} Dallas Cowboy Cheerleader {h}Lakers Girl or {i} Baby-sitter

Seriously never ever apply for one of these; you will have folks talking about you…even if it is a joke.

*****

Just because she let you get some, doesn't mean that you can stay the night. Time to go partna!!! Only exception is if she grabs you by the arm and invite you to stay the night.

*****

No man is to ever wear a shirt with his face on it. Only Prince can do it, and Prince is an 'It" So Prince can do whatever Prince wants to do. Since you are not Prince…YOU CAN'T DO IT!!!

*****

No man is to ever have a "fanny pack", nor any type of pouch. Only tool belts are allowed. If you get caught with this on, be prepared to have it taken and to get beaten by it...just to remind you to NEVER wear it again.

*****

No man is to ever stand in a cheer position, nor any type of stance in which a cheer can break out. You need to have both kneecaps broken if you do this after you have been warned. We bet you won't stand that way ever again...LOL

*****

No man is to ever call his homeboy while he is naked. Said person is to put on some drawers first, at the least. But to be safe, get fully dressed then call your homeboy...this is a first class.

*****

Saying, "No Homo" will not save you from unmanly activities....Breaking a Man Law is frowned upon regardless. If you have to say, "No

Homo" before you do something, then you might wanna reconsider doing it at all. Remember, We are watching you... (evil laugh)

*****

No man is to sit next to another man on a porch swing, unless a case of beer is between them. It can NOT be an off brand beer...You need to be able show one of the big brands...and no arms can have contact at any time while the two men are on said swing.

*****

No man is to scratch another man's back for him....Saying "no homo" won't save you. You must never ask a man to do this, it doesn't matter how bad the itch is. If you are the one asking, then you should be prepared to be stoned in a public place. If your homeboy asks you to do this, you need to punch him in the face, kick him in the ribs, thus taking away his need to have his back scratched.

*****

No man is to ever take professional pictures and hang them on his wall, unless he's a minister or a judge. If you are married and it's a wedding picture next to your wife's wedding picture it is ok. If you are single and you are doing this, you need to break all the toes on your foot...

*****

No man is to ever wear pants so tight, that they're mistaken as baseball pants. Skinny jeans are included in this. No man should never ever wear skinny jeans unless it is a Halloween joke

and the skinny jeans must be taken off after twenty minutes, never to be worn again.

*****

No man is to ever wear wristbands or headbands unless he's getting ready for a game. Walking around with an Iverson jersey on, and a headband and wristband on, makes you look 12.

Did you really need us to tell you this?!?!? C'mon son, so many of you are still doing this and you are above the age of 30. You need to be choked with that headband!!!!

*****

Only Omegas can stick their tongues out in pictures. If you pledged that band fraternity while you were in undergrad, NO...you can't stick out your tongue. You should have been a Man and pledged Que Dog!!!! Violation of this will be a stumping from the Que's while listening to Atomic Dog!!!!

*****

Just because you got a fake grill in your mouth, don't make you hard. Won't nobody hire you with that crap in your mouth. So unless you are a rapper, get that mess out of your mouth before your next job interview. If you need some help we got a hammer and pliers....smh

*****

A man should live by this motto..."Pay your bills, before you pay the bartender."

If your baby mama got to track you down for diapers, wipes, milk, food, or clothes...you are not a baller, so stop acting like one and take care of your children!!! This makes you a real man and baller!!!! If you don't do this, go outside and find the nearest brick and slap your face with it.

*****

To all you dudes riding in your girl's car with your boys, bumping your girl's Nicki Minaj cd, put some gas back in her car, and return it to her immediately. You are fake, a real man has his own car and wouldn't get caught dead listening

to Nicki Minaj or Beyonce in his car!!!! Only exception to this rule is..that it is playing on the

radio and the moment it comes on, you must change the radio station...immediately!!!!! If you have those cd's in your car, let the hood up and slam it on your head!!!!!

*****

Man Laws: Don't Break 'Em

Them tight t-shirts some of y'all dudes wear, can cause suffocation when you try and take it off. Leave them extra smediums on the rack. You know if you have to grunt more than one time putting on a shirt...that ish is way too small...get a different shirt. Trying to look like a muscle man....Yes, we are watching!!!!

*****

Everybody isn't talented enough to be a rapper. Some of y'all got 10 kids. Get a job.
If you have been doing this for more than seven years and no one has picked you up yet, or your not being played on the radio in your own hometown....get a job and retire the fake *** rapper in you!!! Just saying...

*****

If you got jeans so tight, that you can see your calf muscle...burn 'em. You should know they are too tight, you can't even sit down like a man, you are squirming around like a lady with a short dress on just to sit down...take off your left shoe and slap yourself in the eye several times....you know better!!!!

*****

The only thing on your face that should be touched with a razor is your mustache and beard... leave the eyebrows alone. If we see you getting this done...we will come over and bump the person doing it and you will then look like one of those creatures off a Star Trek movie. Don't believe us...try us!!!!

*****

Stop trying to be Diddy in the club when your pockets look like Dylan's, you know him...he is the guy that bags your grocery at your local supermarket. We see you counting up in your

head...you Big Dummy!!!! Opening a tab on a card you know will get declined if you go over 80.00!!!! Stop It!!!!

*****

Stop taking your student loan check and flossing, the moment you are out of money...that lady you have been blowing your money on will move on to the next sucker….oops…we meant guy!!!! Slap yourself three times with a cactus plant…

*****

No man should ever wear a shirt with his nipples showing, nor can he ever wear a shirt that the sleeves fall off his shoulders. You are not in a Broadway play, so stop dressing like you are the star…they got money and can get away with it…you are BROKE and can't!!!!

*****

No man is to ever be hovered over the steering wheel while driving. He must be at least 2 feet back off the wheel. Driving around like a little old lady. You need to turn in your man card if you are ever caught doing this.

*****

No man is to ever scratch his arms, while his palm is turned upwards. Do it and see how crazy it looks…you did it didn't you!!! Now do you see why we said it shouldn't be done by men!!!!

*****

No man is to ever order for his homeboy at a restaurant. Each man must order his own. Wait

on us to order your food… it won't happen here, you better hope we are not done eating if you are not there. If you are there...why in the heck are we trying to order your food anyway!?!?!??!

*****

No man is to ever have his hand under his shirt and rubbing his stomach while talking to another man. Picture that…yeah, we know you almost threw up in your mouth!!! Either he needs to wait until he is by himself to do that or we can kick you in your stomach and give you a reason to rub your stomach. Stop It!!!!!

*****

No man is to ever have "Sex Room" as his ringtone when his homeboy calls. Matter of fact…No Luther Vandross, No Destiny's Child, A real man uses the ring tones on his phone…the ones that Verizon sent it with!!! Nothing more or less…

*****

Unless it's a family picture or family related; no man is to smile while taking a picture with a group of dudes. Even with family don't be showing all of your teeth if you are above the age of 12...Nope...Shouldn't do it!!!!!

*****

No man is to have his house decorated by his accomplishments in the following "sports"..... Cheerleading, Gymnastics, Ribbon Dancing , any type of ballet or dance competitions or Figure Skating, etc. Keep all your "You Got Served" certificates, trophies, and plaques locked up in a safe or burn them. You do not want to have to explain to your son how your did all of those moves in your foolish youth!!! Never show them...let the memories be just that....MEMORIES!!!!!

*****

No man is to ever enter a Wet T-shirt contest. I don't care how much of a bet your boys put on the table....don't you Never, Never, Never, ever, ever, ever...in yo life enter this contest!!!! Someone will have pictures and trust me they will be on social media sooner or later.

*****

NO MAN is to whatsoever, take a bubble bath, unless he is a BOSS like Scarface, and it can't be a regular-sized tub, and he has to have a cigar in his mouth with a TV in the bathroom.

And the bubbles can't be from Bath and Body Works, nor Victoria's Secret.

No…a portable television and a cigarette doesn't count…get you butt out of that small tub with bubbles all on your mama's floor!!!!

*****

NO MAN is to ever have feet smaller than his girls. If you have small feet, you are limited to dating midgets…Yeah we said it…you can't have your girl wearing a size 11 and you are a

size 10 ½….something about that just seems off…

*****

No man is to ever have a bumper sticker that states, I ♥ Kobe. It looks bad even if it is your girl's car. C'mon son…really, think about how crazy that looks. Now if your girl got it and she wants to go see the Lakers without you and she comes back home late…we mean very late at night, jumps in the shower and goes to bed with a smile on her face…well, you know just like we know…just pack up and leave homie….just leave!!!!

*****

No man is to ever highlight anything in pink. We think this one needs no explanation!!!

No man is to ever call the radio station and talk to the D.J. because he gets lonely, or call to apologize live on the air. That requires an automatic butt whipping for 30 straight days…seriously you gonna call in and let everyone hear how you messed up and then begged to be forgiven?!?!??!?!

*****

NO MAN is to have a picture of another man in his wallet. Only ones that get an exemption are Father, son, and grandfather..no uncles, nephews…or cousins.

*****

NO MAN should ever share a drink with another man at the club. If you're too broke to buy your own, maybe you should stay your broke behind at home.....or better yet, get a JOB! One that pays you enough to at least get one drink at the club for yourself. Two punches to the face for both of you for sharing drinks…

*****

No man is to ever buy a birthday cake for another man. Do you see what is wrong with this?!?!? You walk in with a cake, now yo silly self might buy some candles too. We hope you drop the cake and mess it up!!! Buy a six pack of beer or a bottle of his favorite drink, and if he tells you it is wine…you need to reevaluate your friendship…

*****

No man should ever have to take one for the team on his birthday. It's his birthday and someone else should step up and take one for the team…if no one will do it…then look at your friends…or ex-friends as you punch them in the face for messing up your birthday!!!!

*****

No man is to ever call, tell, nor text another man, "I need you right now"....unless he's sinking in quick sand or drowning. If you send this and it is not life or death...be prepared to visit your local hospital...I.C.U is calling your name because you should never panic like a woman and use this...

*****

NO MAN is to ever make physical contact with another man, while a slow song is playing....in a club, at home, etc. Hold all daps, chest bumps, etc. until a rap song comes on. If one of your homeboys tries this...punch him in the eye and kick his knee out of place...this is to save you from people talking about both of you...

*****

NO MAN is to ever ask another man to send him a picture of himself.

We don't even have to explain this one...we hope!!!!!

*****

NO MAN is to ever tell another man a secret. HUH!?!?!
We don't do this either…if you feel the need to gossip, go hang with a bunch of females, guys don't want to talk about secrets…

*****

While taking a pic, no man is to ever say, "cheese". The only way this is done is you are with your young son or daughter and it has to be at Chuck E. Cheese…once you leave…no more saying "Cheese" for pictures.

*****

No man is to ever ask his homeboys for a group hug. This will also cause for a trip to the hospital, the ambulance must come pick you up because none of your male friends will take you in their car for fear of your motives being played out on them... keep your group hug germs to yourself.

No man is to ever forward another man, any of those silly girlish forwards from their cell phones, talkin' bout how much they mean to him. Once you do this and your homeboys walk up to you and slap you with a brick, don't you dare cry...you brought this on yourself. Man up and rub some dirt in your wounds and keep walking.

*****

When you're out to eat, No man is to order before the woman does. Act like you got some form of home training... or get hit with a open hand Ike Turner slap.

*****

No man is to scream like a lil biyotch, when his favorite player is being introduced in the starting lineup. It doesn't matter what sport, NBA, NFL...or college Football or college Basketball. You will be karate chopped in the throat so fast..try it and see what happens!!

If you scream like a little girl, you could be banned from all of your friends houses for a year or more, then you must show them in a public place that you can be cool while watching sports. So a trip to Buffalo Wild wings is in order…before you can hang with the fellas again.

*****

No man is to ever pat his hands together and say, "Yay!". That's ladylike and you should prepare for a serious beat down Mike Tyson style…

Picture that, a guy sitting there clapping his hands together and saying YAY!!!! You go Girl!!! Yeah, we know…punch him in the eye…better yet, punch him in both of his eyes until he stops saying "YAY!!!!"

*****

No man is to ever say, type, or text, "k", as a response. Dude, it's "ok"…that ain't but one more letter to say, type, write, etc. We find that very disturbing. If you are too lazy to type another letter, throw your phone in a local river and don't get another one OK...

*****

No man is to ever share a sofa with another man, while another seating arrangement is available. This goes for your son also if he is over the age of 12, it's cool to show him some love, but you got to get him ready for these rules as well. If you are shaking your head saying my son can sit with me anytime he wants to... slap yourself 4 times in the left eye...

*****

NO MAN is to ever stand or sit in between another man's legs. It is a shame that we even have to put this one in here, but because we have seen it... now we have to warn you. Both of you will get slapped if you both are grown and the other man is not your son under the age of 8... even then you should be telling him to sit next to you.

*****

NO Man is to ever put on Chapstick, like he's putting on lipstick.

WOW, if you see a man doing this, for the sake of all men in this world...slap him so hard that the chapstick is down his throat by his liver in 2.3 seconds!!!!

*****

NO MAN is to ever rub his nipples when he feels horny and letting his woman know it!! She should slap you back into reality. Then call some thugs she knows to slap you again...C'Mon son...Stop IT!!

*****

No man is to ever, and I mean ever, call another man, just to tell him good night. If this is done, it

is time for all of your homeboys to get together and perform a "Code Red" on your butt!!! After 10 hours of beatings, maybe you will think twice about this and never ever think about doing it again!!!

*****

No man is to go jogging in those itty bitty small shorts, you remember the kind like the old greats from yesteryears NBA...You remember those shorts. Some of ya'll men still running in them everyday...Please Stop IT!!! It looks nasty...

*****

NO MAN is to ever dim the lights, in the presence of another man.
Not even to show him how they work, he will just take your word on it...if you insist on showing him and he knocks you out and you wake up 8 hours later with a knot on your head...don't be mad at him, he was protecting himself from YOU!!!

*****

No MAN is to ever call the radio station and dedicate a song to another man. No, You can't even do this for your dad...let your mom, sister, or some other female member of the family do this.

If you do this, this is like the Death Penalty in the N.C.A.A You will try to explain, but it will take you years to get over it…and once you think it is finally over with…someone will remind you that you did this.

***

No man is to ever ask a female the following question: Am I the Biggest and Best Lover you ever had?" You just set your ego up to get crushed if she wants to.

If she says no…. Bobby was the "Biggest" and Steve was the Best, and then she starts smiling really, really, really hard…you just lost your girl and you should feel you ego shrinking at that very moment. Don't ever ask this question ever again, even if she says yes, because she might have lied to save your ego…and next time she might not be nice!!!

*****

No man is to ever take a picture with his face resting on his hands.

Picture that...he got a full beard and mustache but his head is leaning to the right and resting on his hands...Stop it!!!

*****

No man shall ever read ZANE books and brag about it on Facebook. You can read what you want to...just don't be posting about that scene from chapter 3 to everyone that knows you.

*****

NO MAN is to ever have an umbrella that matches his outfit. It needs to be a totally different color. We don't care what the fashion magazines are saying!!! Stop It!!!

*****

NO MAN is to ever call the police 'cause he getting his ass whooped....by his girl. Take it like a man, we hope you stay in the house...at least that way you can lie about who won. If you run

out the house expect it to pop up on WorldStar
or YouTube real soon!!!!

*****

NO MAN, is to ever have a BFF album.
Really just start beating yourself before we
come...it might help out!!! This beating will take
about 22 hours, and we hope to have you in a
comma well before then.

*****

No man is to ever tell his homeboy that he hasn't
seen in a while, that he missed him. It will now
be twice as long before you see him again, and
that's if you ever see him again before one of
you die.

*****

No man is to stand behind another man, and show him how to shoot a gun. That picture is not cool at all, you need to shoot your pinky toe off like right now….and leave!!!

*****

No man is to ever tell his boy, after a workout, "Let's hit the showers". As a man, you never want to hear this from another man. Just go home stank and musty!!!!

*****

No man is to ever bat his eyes.
If you do this, the butt whipping you receive will be well deserved!! No man bats his eyes for nothing, and we mean nothing!!!!

*****

No man is to ever ask his homeboys, what they're getting him for his birthday
If you get nothing at all or a six pack of beer…you just take it and move on…but you should never ask for anything for your birthday…slap yourself in the right eye.

A man must never say, "I'm feeling yucky"...no man is to ever feel "yucky"....

If you have done this..you have violated so many rules, just turn your man card in and not call, text, or see anyone for at least 6 months.

*****

No man is to ever get upset, because he can't find his umbrella, and it's raining.
You better run your sorry butt in the rain and stop crying about an umbrella!!!! You look crazy, looking all over the place for an umbrella and it is a light rain.

*****

If "Secret Lovers" comes on when your homeboy calls you, kill yo self.

You should never call any male if a song comes on, Hell...even the Ques don't call each other

just because Atomic dog comes on!!! Just sit there and enjoy the song, and move it along.

*****

It is NOT okay for 2 men to be in the bathroom at the same time....meaning, NO man is allowed to take a dump, while his homeboy is in the shower!!!!

Men, teach your boys this early on…Don't scar these boys for life.

*****

No man is to ever and I mean ever, throw a baby shower. If you do this, just save the World the trouble and jump out of a 100 story building naked. That sounds better than you throwing a baby shower…

*****

No man is to ever go to school for interior decorating. PERIOD!!!
Just fall on some nails or a big vase…are you serious!?!?!?
*****

No man is to ever walk to the beat of a female song... When Beyonce and Jay Z song Crazy in Love comes on…sit yo BUTT down, there is no need for you to dance, and if you got the dance routine down to a "T"...man card is gone and a trip to the cemetery is in order!!!!

*****

No man is to ever take a picture with a lil ass dog in his lap.

Get yoself a big dog...even if you have a small dog, never ever take a picture with it in your lap!!!!

*****

No man is to ever write like this......"Mi aNd My bEstleS aRe aBouT tO gO HaRd"....kill yo self. That mess is crazy and you need to be shot with buck shots fast!!!! Stop It!!!!

*****

No man is to ever wait for the Wednesday paper, just to clip coupons. We hope you cut your fingers...a lot!!!

*****

No man is to ever ball on a budget. If you're on a budget, it ain't ballin. If you can't afford to impress her, then get back in school...get a better job!!! But then you will see a real woman that is with you, is not there just for the money...but knowing your crazy self...you will go back and get the woman who wants money...and now you are broke again...BIG DUMMY!!!!!

*****

No man is to stand behind another man, and show him how to stroke a pool ball. That's grounds for termination. Turn around and hit him with the stick and walk away dropping the stick. Only requirement is that you break the stick with one swing, if not...then people will look at you crazy!!! So will we...

*****

No man is to ever attempt to make his booty clap. Kill yo self twice…just to be sure…REALLY!!!!!

*****

No man is to ever run away, after his homeboy got stole on and is getting jumped on. You better jump in and help, or that's the end of the homeboyship right there. DON'T EVER DO This…Never!!!! We just might beat you up after the first fight is over…so you better run again…

*****

No man is to ever blow in another man's eye.

REALLY Dude…You better rub your own eye and get whatever might be in there out….We ain't never blowing in your eye, and YOU better not ever ask another man to do it…he might hit you in your eye!!!!

*****

No man is to ever creep up behind another man, and put his hands over his eyes....

You just bought a first class butt whipping...no need to pack...we gonna whip yo butt from Florida to California for doing this...there will be BLOOD!!!!!

*****

No man is to ever rub another man's face, and tell him that he needs to shave.....that's grounds for a beatdown.

Blood and stitches for doing this one...maybe even a cast on your arm or leg!!!

*****

No man is to ever allowed to call himself pretty.

No Pretty Tony...No Pretty Ricky..no nothing...Slap yoself before we get there...

*****

No man is to ever compete in a hoola-hoop contest, if you are drunk and enter… he better not win.

Yeah, picture that your picture at a bar with a trophy for a hoola-hoop contest, which leg do you want to be broken first!?!?!?!

*****

No man is to ever sit or lay on the couch and hug a pillow. That joker is really messed up and no one needs to visit for awhile…like 6 months

*****

No man is to ever place his index finger over another man's lips and tell him to be quiet. That grounds to get shot. We just need to know where the normal hospital you visit because you are going…and fast….Beatdown, shooting, more beating….picture that…ok, now you see why the hospital is in play here….

*****

No man is to ever hold up the Round sign at a boxing match.

It doesn't matter what state or who is boxing, this should never happen!!!!

*****

No man is to sit at home and just eat chocolate after his girlfriend broke up with him.
Get up and get out…go to the club, but never sit there and sulk like a girl…it is not for a MAN to do!!!!

*****

No man is to have a tool belt on with some cut-off shorts...matter of fact, shorts period.
Again, The Village People are not relevant anymore…please stop your friends from doing this.

*****

No man is ever own a thigh master. Another clear violation, and we should not have to explain this…but of course there are too many men out there using and hiding one of these in their closets. STOP IT!!!

*****

No man is to ever fix another man a glass of wine, unless he's working at a restaurant. You will look like a plum fool pouring another man a glass of wine at your house. You need to grab him a beer or a shot glass!!!

*****

NO man is to take a picture with his head tilted to the side. If you see one of your boys doing this…punch him in the throat and we hope that makes him lean his head the right way….Straight up!!!

*****

No man is to ever say, "let me get comfy". If one of your boys say this or something close to it, you need to punch him so hard that his kidney releases all fluids. No man should never say something like this!!!!

*****

No man is to ever like a team, because of the team's colors. Each man should know something about his team, it shouldn't matter if it is baseball, basketball, or football. If your friend says he like the Heat, Bears, or Braves because of their colors…go to your local corner store buy a bag of ice…take it back to his house and swing it at his head…he needs shock treatment and you are doing the world a favor!!!!

*****

No man should ever have a status with a heart in it, nor any other symbols. Another moment in Man Law history that should not have to be stated, but because we have seen it too many times, Guys please stop doing this….

*****

No man is to ever clean up his place, with Sade blasting, or any other female R&B singer. Doing this will get a broom slapped across your head.

You…yeah you…you know you were doing this.
We won't put you on blast, but please stop it!!!

*****

No man is to ever watch a porno with another
dude. No need to even explain this…even if
your boy says, you got to see this lady…take it
home and watch it by yoself!!!

*****

No man is ever allowed to cry at his homeboy's
wedding; unless he's giving the Best Man's
speech....that is all.
No, nothing else fits in the situation…don't even
try it…Never!!!!

*****

No man is to ever try out to be an NFL, NBA, or
any other sport, cheerleader, nor on the dance
line. If you are caught on the showing of this on
cable and we catch you…get ready we will break
both of your legs!!! Tonya Harding style!!!!

*****

No man is Never to put on Destiny's Child Cater to you when his homeboy(s) come over. Not even the live version from the Old Bet Awards show…We don't care how fine they look in those dresses.

*****

Sharing Chapstick is not cool, and no man is never to ask let me borrow yours. No two men's lips should touch the same chapstick…open or unopened!!!

*****

No man is to ever tell another man, to come over because he's bored or lonely. If one of your boys does this…get in your car…drive to his house, get your bat as you get out of the car and break his arm. I bet he is not bored anymore, and NO…you can't take him to the hospital!!!

*****

No man is to never walk around with a shirt with
no bottoms on. A wife beater and socks
shouldn't be your wardrobe. If these are all the
clothes you have, then you need to just walk off
a cliff right now…it needs to be a closed casket
because you don't have any clothes
remember…

*****

It is not okay to have a man crush on a pro
athlete, celebrity, or any man period.
If we have to explain this…then you are lost and
we can only hope you find your way back to us!!!
Leave your man card at the window please.

*****

No man is ever to allowed to say, "Ooh, this is
my song", and then proceed to turn the radio up.
If you are riding with your friend when he does
this, you must immediately ask him to pull over,
get out of the car and catch a taxi back to your
house.

*****

No man is ever allowed to lip-sync an R&B song, especially with head movements. Two or three slaps to the back of the head should fix this, if not give him one punch to the throat and give it 20 seconds…he should be ok after this ok!!!

*****

Don't try and turn it up, when your pockets are turned down...stay home. Watch some youtube videos but whatever you do…don't go out broke!! Women can do this…a GROWN man can NOT!!!!!

*****

If your homeboys tell you something for your own good about a female.... don't go back to that female and tell her what they told you. Next time, they ain't tellin' you nothing,
and for acting like a little girl they should whip your butt just because…..

*****

If you buy a female a drink, that doesn't mean that you can stalk her all night. If your game wasn't tight enough to catch her…walk away and chalk that 15.00 drink to the game. You should have talked to her first before buying the drink…We bet you lose hundreds of dollars in the club every weekend don't you.

*****

If you have a girly name, you have to go by your initials...like J.C. or T.B. or something like that. Never tell anyone what your real name is…if your boys know it, they will only clown you in private and not in public. If one does it, punch him in the throat fast!!!

*****

After a good physical session with your lady, you should not be the one cooking grits and cheese eggs!!! Only exception to this rule is that it's her birthday or mother's day. If it is not one of these days, you need to be karate chopped in the throat!!!

*****

No man, is to ever tell his homeboy, "Good night". "Holla at you in the morning dawg" is sufficient enough. If your boy says this…look at him like you have been constipated for 100 years and if he doesn't fix it fast…whip his butt right away…

*****

Under no circumstances are two men to take a picture with their cheeks touching. We mean face cheeks or any other cheeks!!! Don't get caught face to face with another dude!!! Not a good look at all….No it can't be family unless your father and son…nothing else will be excused!!

*****

No man is allowed to give up his jacket to his homeboy, because his homeboy said that he is cold. He deserves to freeze his butt off for not bringing his own coat.

*****

No man should ever get mad because he missed the season finale of America's Top Model. He shouldn't be even watching it in the first place. If he ever admits this in a public setting…he deserves whatever punishment is dished out including all butt whippings, karate chops, and punches to the face!!!

*****

No man is to beat up on neither women nor children. If said action is witnessed, then you have the right to go "ham" on the person. Shots to the nuts are approved.
If he blocks the shots to the nuts..go to the face…then back to his nuts and let the lady get in a couple of shots as well!!!

*****

No man should ever get his belly-button pierced. Another simple rule that you would think we shouldn't have to explain, but of course…we have to tell you!!! If it is ever suggest "Let's get our belly-button pierced" punch whatever guy said this, knock him down and leave him right where he fell!!!

*****

No man should ever shave his legs unless he's on the Olympic swim team competing against Michael Phelps. Picture this…you walk in the bathroom and your man is shaving his legs!!! What are you shaving them for?!?!?! Really…

*****

No man should have any facial piercings....You ain't Tupac. What is the purpose of this?!?!? Really, we need to know.

*****

No man shall get his nipples pierced unless he's a drummer in a rock band.
You're not even the drummer at your church, so why do you want your nipples pierced?!?!?! SMH….

*****

If you're performing a dance routine, (which we are highly against), you must not start your dance off by doing a spin-around. You need to do some of MC Hammers moves.

*****

Waiting outside your girl's residence, crying with a pistol, waiting to see who comes out of her apartment is lame. Think about it...is it really worth it? NOPE, we know you are thinking of all the things that she did to you and now she is doing it to him and he is enjoying it...wait, that wasn't helpful....lmbo just leave ok

*****

NO man shall ever order a Pizza slice with no meat on it. Seriously you need to put something on your veggie slice because all of us just lost 3 years of respect for you by you doing this!!!!

*****

NO man must have a keychain with a heart on it.

If you got a problem with this, then you need to get rid of your little heart on your key chain!!!! Then everyone will stop looking at you.

*****

Riding in your car bumpin' to Trina is a no-no...we don't care how hard she may be...you are a MAN and should not be bumping her music in your car like that!!! Switch to something else...NOW!!!!

*****

While on vacation sharing a hotel room/suite with your boys is ok to save money, but put your damn draws on in the bathroom! No nakedness!

*****

Also about vacation... If you or your homeboys hit the beach, neither lying out nor sitting on towels together is cool. Please get your own or sit on the sand!!! No you can't sit on a corner of the towel either...

*****

Men must not be in the Jacuzzi together without women. There are no passes or exceptions to this rule, if your homeboy comes and tries to get in,....look at him like he done lost his damn mind. If he still gets in, you have to get out immediately but punch him in the eye after you get out!!!

*****

If you ran out of clean underwear, you better hit up the nearest Wal-Mart or free-ball, 'cause ya ain't borrowing none. No grown man should be asking to borrow some anyway…karate kick him in the ribs for even asking that…

*****

If you sleep with your hands in between your knees, you need them cut off. We will bring the saw; please don't run…we will catch you!!!

*****

Jeans without back pockets will not be tolerated, what man does this!!! Yeah, if it is you…go to your closet and throw them away…NOW!!!!

*****

Riding around in your girl's car, trying to look hard, with her sorority tag on the front ain't cool. Park it in the driveway immediately. Get yo own ride…NOW!!!

*****

No swimming with the lil floaters around your arm. We will pop them and then attempt to push you in the deep end, so you can learn how to swim!!!

*****

If you got taco meat on your chest, cover it up or shave that crap. Walking around looking like Magnum P.I. ain't cool. Really, the 80's are gone…STOP IT!!!

*****

If your ass is over 12, no Easter-egg hunting for you, my bruh. Unless you're looking for the golden egg with the $20 bill and you need some gas money…then all bets are off…knock them kids down!!!!

*****

We better not see any of y'all grown asses up saying an Easter speech. We might be at your church, you never know. We are bringing bats and hammers…we are breaking something…

*****

If your son is older than 6, and asks to take a picture with the Easter bunny, that when shit gets real. Get him a Batman toy or some G.I. Joe's…..Buy him a baseball bat…do something for the sake of your son!!

*****

If you get you some this weekend, the neighbors should not know her name. They should only know yours. Do we need to repeat this one…if she got you yelling her name, C'Mon son…flip it somehow…someway!!!

*****

When running for whatever reason, a guy should never have his arms flailing around like a lil b*tch. Run like a man. You better run like the old Carl Lewis did…act like the police coming for you…

*****

Every man must act like MacGyver around his woman. Even if you don't know how to fix it, at least act like you know what you're doing. Just start flipping wires and moving stuff around, she will get excited and maybe …just maybe give you some extra time because you tried so hard to fix it.

*****

No man is allowed to own a dog that he can fit into his pocket. No Questions… if you ask, we will beat you down!!!

*****

If your son decides to join the band, he must stay away from the flute/clarinet family. If he insists on going this way… slap him with a tube… then gut check him with a trombone… We bet he change his mind fast…

*****

There shouldn't be 4 dudes to a booth in Waffle House. 3 dudes and a female is cool, but 4 dudes ain't gonna cut it. You must either sit at the high-counter or at the tables. We suggest you be the one sitting next to the female… that way, if legs touch it won't be awkward!!!!

*****

No man is allowed to shine on his homeboy in the presence of his lady. That's viewed as hating. All the fellas will jump you when she leaves…don't run…don't run!!

*****

If you can't hoop, don't sign the list. If you were the water boy in high school and college…just hope you get picked.

*****

No man is allowed to have a neither blowup poster nor picture of himself or any other man on his bedroom wall. You are not 10 and you should not act like it. Punch yourself in the face…5 times for this mess!!!!

*****

If you go to the strip club, you're not allowed to make it rain, then pick it back up when she isn't looking. Stay yo broke self at home, we hope the bouncer punches you in the kidney and you pee in your clothes for doing that stupid ish right there!!!

*****

When taking a picture, you cannot, and I mean NOT, take a picture with your back turned and looking over your shoulder. Matter of fact, you can't be turned sideways either. No over-the-shoulder looking…matter fact…look over this way…we will slap you with a shovel…right in your face for doing these poses!!!

*****

You may not talk on the phone to your boy while you're soaking in the tub... (and you're only allowed to soak, if you're using Epsom salt).

*****

You are not allowed to talk to your boy on the phone, while lying on your stomach, facing away from the TV. Picture that!! WOW, turn yo monkey self around and get off your stomach!!

*****

Fighting another guy over a woman, who is not your wife, is a no-go. Especially if she looks like Ben Wallace.

*****

Drinking wine while the rest of your boys are drinking beer is a negative. You won't be invited next time, we promise you. You will see them out and look around the table…they will lie to help you save face…and next time, you still won't be invited!! Watch…

*****

If your son dots his "i" with a circle or a heart, then it's time to have a man-to-man talk. Bring a Playboy magazine with you to have the visual aids.

*****

Unless you are Superman or a crime-fighter, you are not allowed to rest your fists on your hips. Please don't do it….we did say please, running upstairs to put your underwear on the outside and then doing it doesn't count!!! A Baseball Bat to your legs is coming…

*****

When riding down the street, two men cannot share the arm rest. Armrest goes to the driver…

*****

Not only is ordering dessert when out with the homies is strictly prohibited, but if two homeboys are out and one orders dessert, then that makes it a date. NO Desserts!!! You will get kicked in the jaw if you try!!!!

*****

No man is to ever sleep in a t-shirt and draws (drawers)…put on some damn shorts.

*****

Yogurt is strictly prohibited. PERIOD!!!!

*****

Men don't comb their hair. You brush it, pick it, twist and lock it, or get up and go. Please don't ever say this again.

*****

If you are a woman beater, you need to get stoned, like in the old days...not jail-time, but lined-up against a wall and stoned by the best arms in the business. Guys like Peyton Manning, Tom Brady, Donovan McNabb, Drew Brees, etc. and between each person throwing stones we will patch you up so that the stoning takes longer...You need to know what it feels like...

*****

No man is to ever go to the gym just to attend aerobics class. We will sit outside with any stones left over and throw them at you, try us...we dare you!!!!

*****

Buying the new Usher album on the release date is unacceptable. PERIOD!!!!!!

*****

Before you get into someone's face, do a self-breath test. Blow into your hand, and if it smells like a dirty diaper, take a rain check from talking to that person, and save yourself the embarrassment. If your breath burns the hairs on your face, what do you think it will do to the other person?!?!?!?! This is a Brick hitting offense!!!

*****

If your homeboy seriously dated her, then she's off limits. We don't have to explain this one....We hope not!!!!

*****

If you brag about "it" to a woman, then you better back it up. Don't sell yourself "short"...literally. She will be mad and put you on blast...and if we hear about it…we will laugh, we won't spread it anymore than it has already gone, but you might need to move to another city and state!!!!!

*****

All men must teach their daughters the "Kung-Fu" grip, just in case guys get out of line. Then run tell daddy, brother, uncle, or cousins and we will take care of the rest!!!

*****

If your rims cost more than your car, then use the rim money for a down payment on a new car. Stop being a boy and grow up…

*****

Your Halloween costume should never consist of: a bumble bee, tooth fairy, go-go dancer, or flight attendant. Be prepared for an ugly beating and because it is Halloween, no one is calling the police!!!!

*****

If you have a son, it is not permissible for him to play in his mama's makeup bag, nor walk around in her heels. If said action is done, you are to immediately punch him in the chest and sign him up for football.

*****

At karaoke night, you must sing a manly song, and not "I Will Survive". What kind of flowers do you want at your funeral?!?!?! Let us catch you…yup this is the DEATH PENATLY!!!!!

*****

No, you can't join your woman and her friends for Margarita Night. What kind of tampons do you use!?!?! Let that lady have some breathing room WITHOUT you…real men, give her money and tell her to have a good time!!!

*****

Under no circumstances should any household that consists of all males, have American Idol on any Television in the house.

*****

Being part of a singing group and wearing colored contacts, automatically forfeits your man rights. No, you have to wait for 5 years to even apply to get them back!!!

*****

If you watched male figure-skating during the Olympics, climb on top of your roof and jump off. You better not cry after landing either...man up ...JUMP FOOL!!!!!

*****

Toothpaste, mouth wash, lotion, deodorant, cologne and after-shave are the only toiletries that a man should have. Not face cream, fruity smelling lotion, nor excessive hair products. If you have these...run and go play in traffic...L.A Traffic at that!!!!

*****

When holding hands with another man at the altar call at church, your fingers should not be locked with his...matter of fact, when the preacher says "amen", you have less than 1 second to let go of his hand. If he tries to hold your hand longer...you have a right to punch him in the face!!!!

*****

"Sex In the City" nor "Girlfriends" should not be in your TV. watching routine. We have a bat, we can bring it over if you don't feel like punching yourself in the face!!!!

*****

Every man should know at least 2 players off the following Pro Teams....Celtics, Lakers, Cowboys, Eagles, Yankees, and Steelers...past or present!!!! Yeah, we see you trying...learn those names fool!!!!!

*****

No man should ever have a pink or leopard-print phone. Really...really...hey bruh, let me hold your bat to whip you with!!!!

*****

The only time a man lips should be greasy, is when he's eating chicken. Get the hint...we hope you do!!!!

*****

If you ever cried at a Michael Jackson, Luther Vandross, Prince, or Jagged Edge concert, then your man card has expired. Please deposit it in any local mailbox...it will be returned to us, and NOPE you can't have it back!!!

*****

No man, shall ever roll his neck.
NEVER....EVER!!! We will try to break it for you if you are doing this....

*****

If you go on American Idol or Sunday's best, you shall never sing a song, that was originally performed by a woman..i.e. "New Attitude" by Patti LaBelle, or "What's Love Got To Do" by Tina Turner.

*****

If singing in the church choir, stay away from the tambourines. Don't even stand close to anyone playing it, they might ask you to play it that Sunday that Sister Jenkins is out because she broke her hip!!!! Heck naw!!!!!

*****

NO MAN is to ever take pole-dancing classes, matter fact, no man to ever swing from a pole, unless he is a fire-fighter....if we come in the strip club and see you doing a dance and shaking something for some change....we are whipping your butt right there on stage...then taking your money to buy beers with until the police come...

*****

No Man is to ever feel another man's head, to see if he has a fever. Yeah, picture that…a grown rub touching your head to see if you are hot…go take a shower with some boiling grits!!!!

*****

If you bathe with body wash, it better have "For Men" on there…unless it's a manly brand like Old Spice or Lava. Now, Lever 2000 gets a pass, but it has to be the original kind.

*****

It is so disrespectful to take a dump while another man is in the shower. That's fighting action. However, you only get a pass if the shower owes you money or has slept with your sister. Then those actions have been justified, and if that is the case…then no courtesy flushes either…

*****

When a man is on the toilet… that is his "ME TIME". Don't try to attempt to strike up a

conversation through the door. He and his
stomach are having a moment. They are trying
to make peace. Leave them be or get your arms
and legs broke...picture how stupid you
look...hope the fumes knock you out!!!

*****

Butt crumbs or pee stains/dribbles on the toilet is
a justified cause to get pistol whipped. Hospital
time for you...do you want me to call your
mother and let her know what hospital?!?!?!

*****

Shaving balls and leaving hair in the sink or
around the sink ... is a just cause to break a
lease AND break the shaver's jaw. Lock the
door, we should never walk in and see this....but
before you leave clean it up...or you will be
cleaning blood up.

*****

While at the strip club, no she doesn't love you,
she just loves your tax money. Spend wisely.
Fool....Going around thinking Bubbles loves
me!!!! Damn Fool....

*****

No, you cannot take a woman that's not your wife, daughter, girlfriend, or female relative shopping and splurge on them. Now, if you're doing it for someone that's less fortunate, then that's something different, therefore, I applaud you. But doing it to get the drawls is nothing short of 'SAD".

*****

If you're over 30, it's too late to be buying your first set of speakers for your car. SERIOUSLY!!! Don't do it…

*****

No, you cannot turn into the local weed man just because you have tax money… just leave it to the "experts". You are about to go to jail and become the girlfriend of some dud that is 6'6 and 400 pounds…no crying at night when he wants to snuggle…you knew you were not a weed man in the first place…Sleep tight with Bubba!!!!

www.ingramcontent.com/pod-product-compliance
Lightning Source LLC
Chambersburg PA
CBHW071720040426
42446CB00011B/2151